WHAT IS A ROBOT?

Contents

Written by Adrian Bradbury

Collins

What is a robot?

A robot is a machine that can be given instructions by a computer to do different tasks.

You need lots of **experts** to make a robot: people who are good at building things (engineers), people who are good with computers (computer scientists) and people who are good at maths.

Do all robots look like people?

This is the first robot to look like a human. It was built in 1927 and it's called Herbert!

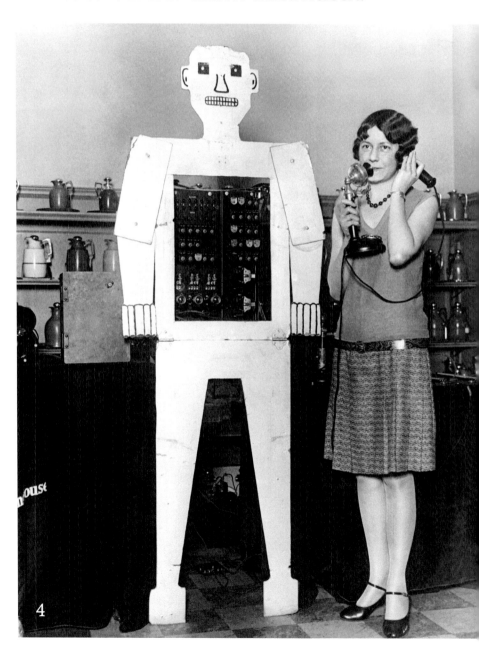

This modern robot has been built to look and move like a real person. It can walk and run, and even hop on one leg, but most robots don't look like people.

Robots can carry out lots of different actions and jobs to help us. This robot arm can pack things in boxes. It has been built to do this job, but it doesn't need to look like a person to do it.

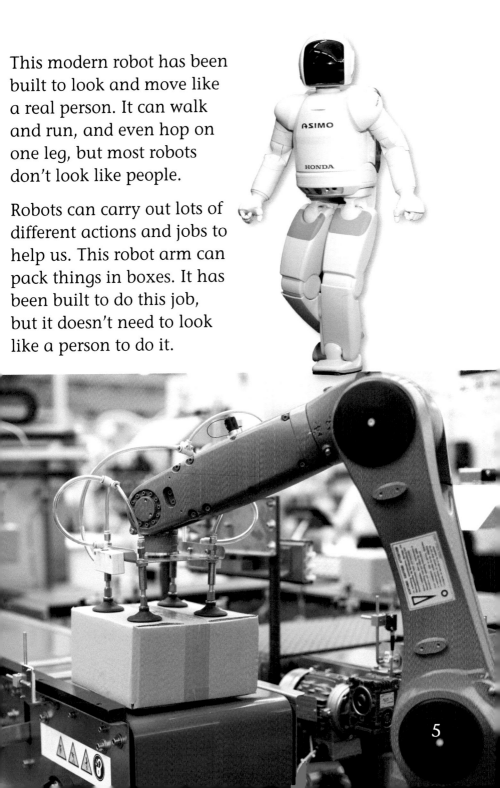

Can robots think?

Robots can only use information that we put into them with a computer. We call this "programming" them. The more information we put in, the more things a robot can do, and the more choices it can make. In this sense, they can "think", but in a limited way.

Your programming has been going on ever since you were born. You're **constantly** storing information in your brain. This comes from things you see, hear, touch, taste and feel. It comes from what you read, what people tell you, and from the things that happen to you in life. That gives you a big head start on a robot.

Robots can be programmed to learn and solve problems – how to play chess, for example. But, unlike humans, robots can't think for themselves ... yet.

Can robots see and touch?

A robot can be given eyes that are just as powerful as human eyes. They'll never grow tired or need to blink. The challenge is for the robot to understand what it's seeing. If you saw a lion walking towards you, licking its lips, you would think, "Yikes! Run away!" A robot might just see "Lion: brown four-legged mammal" and ignore it.

Our sense of touch warns us of dangers. Our skin can feel pain if something is too hot, or if something is pressing too hard on it. Scientists are now working on special "skins" for robots that can sense the same things. This will allow them to be more like humans, and work **alongside** people safely.

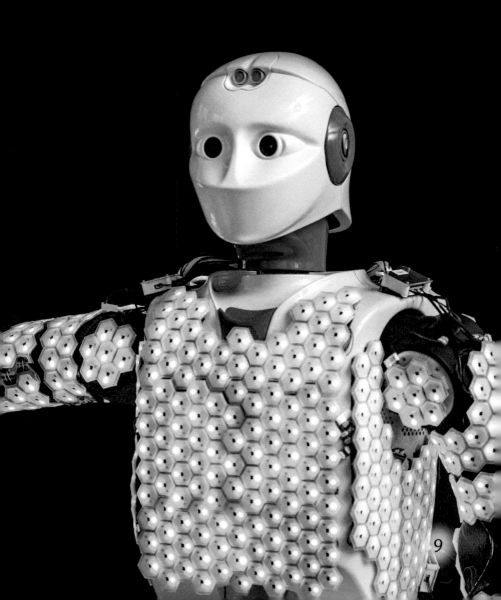

Can robots be creative?

Yes! Say hello to Ai-da, the robot artist. She has a special robotic eye that helps to guide her robotic arm.

Robots can already play a range of musical instruments, including drums, violin and trumpet. They can also be programmed to **compose** their own music. However, people often write music about human experiences such as happy or sad events. When you listen to music, you can feel the **emotion** in the words and sounds. A robot doesn't have these emotions or experiences, so it can't express them in music.

A robot can watch a **3D** video and copy the actions to cook a very tasty meal. But the ingredients must be carefully laid out for the robot to use. And if you swapped marmite for cream, a robot wouldn't know the difference. It can't taste the meal to decide if it needs more salt, and it can't find the salt where someone put it – right at the back of the cupboard!

Will robots take over human jobs?

Robots already do some jobs that humans used to do. In car factories, robots are programmed to do a lot of the **repetitive** jobs needed to **assemble** a car. A robot can drill holes much faster and more accurately than a human. Its arm can't slip so it can't hurt itself in the machinery. It won't get bored, tired or sick, and it won't need a tea break (or a holiday every summer!). Robots are 24-hour super-workers, 365 days of the year.

Have you ever wondered who put those lovely juicy apples in that plastic wrapper? The chances are it was a robot. But … if you put 20 apples in front of a robot, it couldn't tell which ones are going off, or have bugs in them. You need a human to do that job before the apples can be packed by a robot.

Will I ever have a robot teacher?

Possibly. Robot teachers could be programmed with all the information needed to teach whole classes of children of any age. They could switch from a class of six-year-olds to a class of 16-year-olds without difficulty, or from a History lesson to a Maths lesson. They would be able to give each child different tasks to fit their ability or understanding.

But would a robot teacher be able to sense when you're having a bad day, and sit down with you for a little chat? Could they move you to a different table if you're not getting on with someone? Probably not.

Will there be robot doctors and nurses?

Robots are already used to work out what's wrong with you if you tell them all your **symptoms**, and they can be programmed to find the right treatment for your problem. Robots are also used for some operations. A doctor watches a screen and moves levers, while the robotic arms carry out the work. A robot's "fingers" are very **precise**, and they never slip or drop anything.

But a doctor has many skills that a robot doesn't have yet. A doctor can examine someone who isn't well and work out what's wrong with them without knowing all the patient's symptoms. A doctor can listen to a patient's voice and sense their worries and fears. No robot can do this yet.

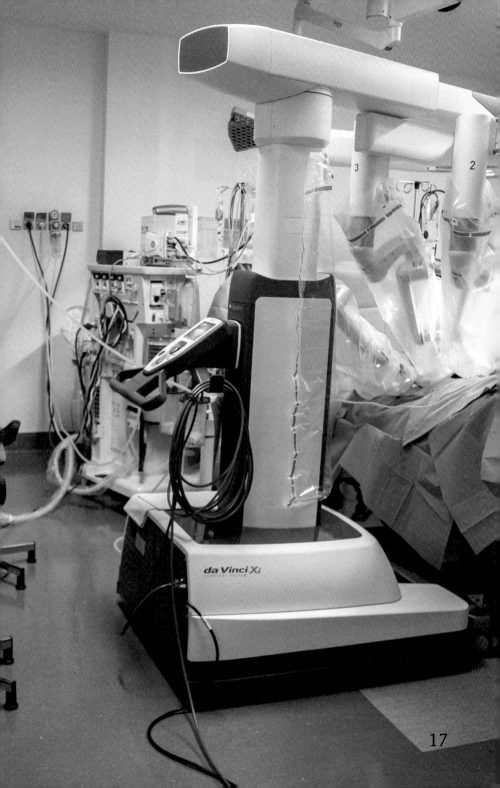

Can robots drive?

Cars are already being tested that can drive themselves without the help of a human. They have sensors that help them to avoid other road users or pedestrians, and their computer brain will speed the car up when the road is empty, or slow down if it's wet or foggy.

This robot, called IVO, can sit in the driving seat and drive a car just like a human would. Its three arms operate the steering wheel, while its robotic feet work the pedals.

Can robots fly?

Yes! There's a special type of robot called a drone. It's like a tiny helicopter that can be programmed to fly or **hover** in the air. Drones contain cameras that can take films from above or help to search for missing people. They are much cheaper than helicopters and can fit into much tighter spaces.

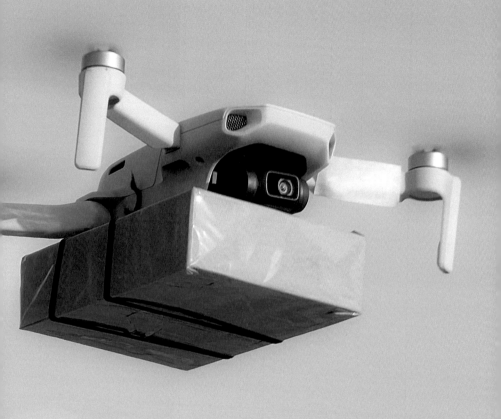

Drones can also be used to deliver food or medicines after disasters such as earthquakes. Some companies already use drones to deliver parcels to your doorstep. They save money on drivers and fuel, and they won't get held up in a traffic jam!

Can I have a robot pet?

It depends how lifelike you want your robot to be. This robot dog is called SPOT. It can run and climb stairs, but at $74,000 (nearly £60,000) it's very expensive! And, of course, it looks and feels nothing like a real dog.

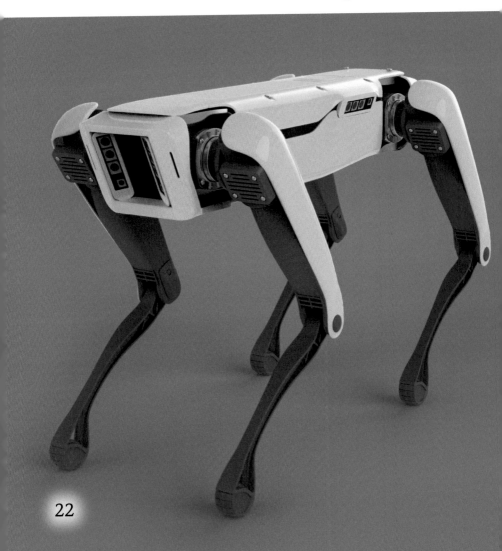

Scientists are working hard to make skin and hair more realistic. Who knows, one day soon you may have your very own RoboCat. It will have silky fur just like a real cat, in any colour you choose.
On the command "JUMP!" it will leap up on to your lap and will be programmed to purr whenever you stroke it. An app on your phone will track it so it can't get lost. Just press a key and your RoboCat will return to base straight away, ready to be cuddled.

If you want a cat like this, you'll have to wait for it to be invented.

Can I become a robot?

You can't become a robot, but robotic arms, hands, legs and feet have been made for people who need them.

Doctors had to remove both of Tilly Lockey's hands and lower arms when she was a baby. Now she has new robotic arms, built by a **3D printer**. The muscles and nerves in her upper arms can make the robot arms and fingers move.

Scientists have even managed to link a robot's movements directly to a person's brain.
This man's brain is connected to a computer.
Using just his thoughts, he's able to take part in a virtual race, and can steer using brain signals.
How amazing is that!?

Sensors are attached here. The sensors record the man's brainwaves and send a message to the robot.

What's the future for robots?

Scientists believe that they'll be able to programme a group of robots to work together to rescue people who are in danger, maybe on a mountain or in a jungle. The robots will be capable of cooperating with each other to move objects and give first aid.

Gradually, new science may mean robots will look and move more like humans. Robots will become cheaper to make, so lots of people might own one. They could be controlled by speaking or thinking, so you'll just have to say the command: "Robot, tidy my room!" and your own personal robot will do it for you.

But, beware! By then, robots may be able to think for themselves. Your robot might just fold its arms and reply: "Sorry, no tidying until your homework's done!"

This robot, called Perseverance, is exploring Mars and sending back pictures to scientists on Earth!

So, *that's* what robots are!

27

Glossary

3D three-dimensional, so you can see an object's height, width and depth

3D printer a machine that can print out objects, rather than just paper

alongside next to

assemble build, put together

compose make up, or write

constantly all the time

emotion feeling

experts people who know a lot about something, or can do it really well

hover stay in one place in the air

precise exact

repetitive a task that you do over and over again

symptoms signs that tell you something may be wrong

Index

Spot the robot

worker

painter

teacher

driver

doctor

musician

pet

player

postal worker

Ideas for reading

Written by Christine Whitney
Primary Literacy Consultant

Reading objectives:
- retrieve information from non-fiction
- be introduced to non-fiction books that are structured in different ways
- explain and discuss their understanding of books

Spoken language objectives:
- ask relevant questions
- speculate, imagine and explore ideas through talk
- participate in discussions

Curriculum links: Design and technology: design – research the design of innovative, functional products, aimed at particular individuals or groups; Writing: write for different purposes

Word count: 1631

Interest words: compose, emotion, hover, 3D printer, sensors

Resources: recyclable resources, such as clean, empty yoghurt pots, boxes, card etc

Build a context for reading

- Ask children to stand up and move like a robot! Discuss with them why they chose those movements and what they know about robots.
- Read the title of the book and ask children to discuss this question. What do they expect to read about in this book?
- Challenge children to ask three questions about robots. When reading the book, children should see if their questions are answered.

Understand and apply reading strategies

- Read to page 6. Ask children to explain what it means to *programme* a robot.
- Continue to read to page 11. We read that robots *can also be programmed to compose their own music.* Ask children to discuss why a robot can't express emotion through that music.
- Read pages 20 and 21 together and ask children to identify three ways in which drones can be used.
- Look closely at the contents page. What does it tell the reader? How is this different from the index?